Lila and Andy learn about

Smart Cities

Kenneth Adams

Book Cover by Kenneth Adams
Illustrations by Kenneth Adams
First Edition 2025

ISBN: 978-1-998552-13-9

Not all mistakes lead to failure.
Some take you exactly where you are
meant to be.

Hi there! We're Lila and Andy, and we love discovering how the world around us works.

Today, we want to tell you about smart cities and all the cool ways technology makes our neighborhoods safer, cleaner, and more fun to live in.

Engineers, scientists, city planners, and community members work together by using new technology to make systems that help cities run smoothly.

Buses that use technology to make sure they're running on time, streetlights that switch on and off by themselves to save energy, and traffic lights that change based on how many cars are waiting are only a few of the things that keep smart cities functioning well.

A smart city connects everything, and all its systems work together to make our lives easier. It's like living in the future!

Smart commuter buses are almost always on time.

Cars that drive themselves are less prone to accidents.

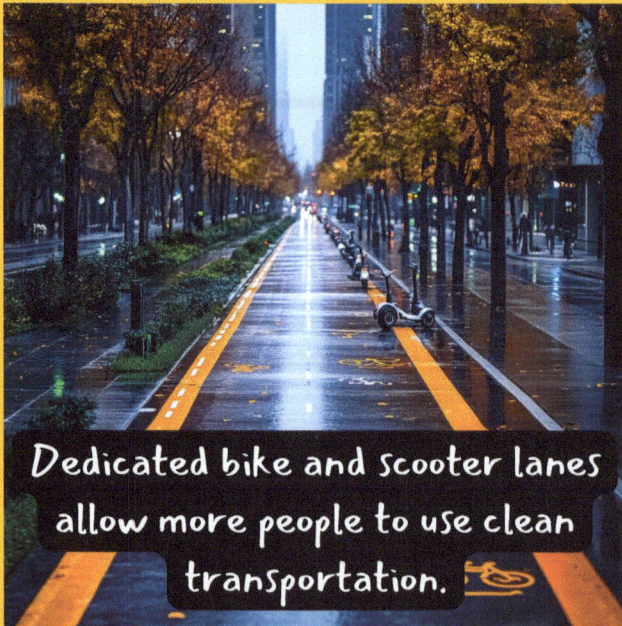

Dedicated bike and scooter lanes allow more people to use clean transportation.

Smart train systems can operate safely with no help from people.

TRANSPORTATION

The main goal of using smart technologies when it comes to transportation is to relieve traffic congestion and reduce noise and air pollution.

Buses and trains have computers that track their location and adjust schedules based on how much traffic there is.

Self-driving vehicles use cameras and sensors to make sure they drive safely. They can also talk with traffic signals and use navigation applications to find the fastest routes.

Some cities have separate roads or lanes for electric bikes and scooters, making it easier for people to use vehicles that don't create pollution.

In Copenhagen, they've installed sensors in bike lanes that detect when groups of cyclists are approaching traffic lights. The system automatically changes the signals to give priority to bikes, especially during rush hour or rainy weather, making cycling more convenient.

Smart transportation systems make travel safer and easier for everyone, especially those who can't drive.

GREEN BUILDINGS

Green buildings are designed to be kind to the environment. They have smart windows that help regulate indoor temperatures by reducing heat loss during winter and keeping the building cool during summer.

Some buildings use sensors to adjust window shutters, lights, and smart thermostats automatically.

These systems turn off lights in empty rooms, open windows when fresh air is needed, and regulate the inside temperature to avoid using too much heating fuel or electricity for air conditioners.

This prevents cities from wasting energy while helping the environment.

Did you know that some smart cities have public art installations that react to environmental conditions, changing their colors or shapes accordingly?

Public parks allow people living in big cities to enjoy the outdoors.

Smart technologies make special events super fun.

Did you know that in smart cities, public parks are transformed into "smart parks" with interactive digital installations, solar-powered Wi-Fi, and sensors that monitor air quality to create safer, more engaging green spaces?

PUBLIC SPACES

Tech helps smart cities make public spaces better for everyone. Sensors count how many people hang out in parks, plazas, and playgrounds. This helps city planners figure out where they need more benches, trees, or play equipment.

During major events, smart systems can help manage crowds. They can suggest routes that aren't packed and make sure emergency exits are clear.

Overhead sensors forming part of an Automated Parking Guidance System indicate where available parking spots are.

Paying for parking at a digital pay machine saves time and money.

PARKING

Finding parking in a smart city is easy thanks to special sensors that know which parking spots are empty. Mobile apps guide drivers directly to available spaces, reducing the time spent driving around looking for parking.

With smart parking meters, you can pay with your phone or card, and you can even add more time to your meter from wherever you are! This makes parking way easier and cuts down on traffic from cars driving around looking for a spot.

Smart street lights are connected to special sensors, cameras, and the internet. They adjust their intensity and brightness automatically and can switch on and off depending on how busy traffic is.

LIGHTING

Street lights in smart cities don't just light up the streets. They use motion sensors to brighten when people are nearby and dim when no one is around, saving energy.

Some smart lights can change colors to signal emergency routes or guide people to special events.

These lights also collect information about air quality, and their built-in cameras can help find lost pets or spot problems like accidents, making streets safer for everyone.

In Barcelona, smart lampposts are equipped with LED bulbs that save energy, sensors that measure air quality, and WiFi hotspots that provide free internet. They even have sensors that can detect if a parking space is empty and help drivers find parking through an app.

Rainwater collection is a smart and simple way to preserve precious water.

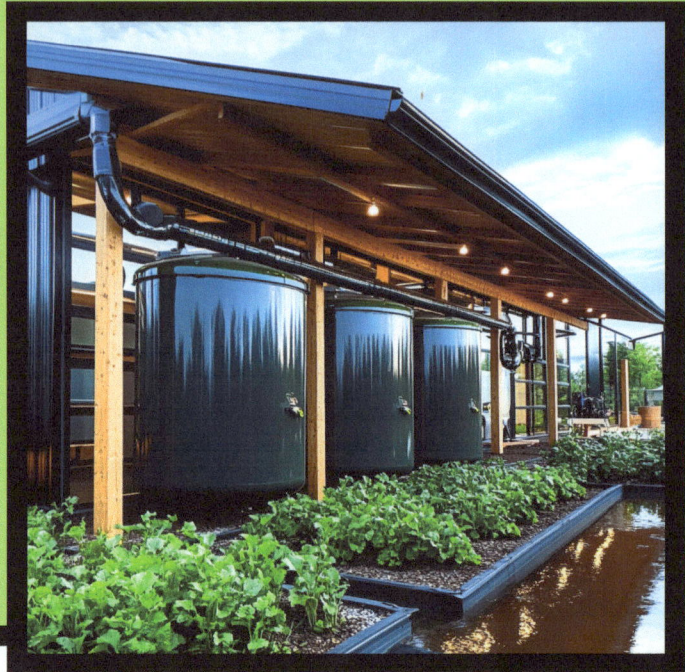

Smart water meters measure how much water you use and let you know when there's a leak.

WATER MANAGEMENT

Water is precious in all cities. In smart cities, special sensors monitor water quality and how much water is used. They can also detect water leaks very early, preventing water from being wasted.

Smart irrigation systems in parks and gardens check soil moisture and weather forecasts to water plants only when needed.

Some buildings collect rainwater for toilets and garden watering, saving clean drinking water for other purposes.

Smart water meters help people understand how much water they use. This allows them to manage their water use and reduce wasting water.

Singapore has a ton of sensors all over its water system that can find leaks right away. They also have smart water meters in homes that let people track their water use on an app. The city's Marina Barrage, a dam in the city center, stores freshwater and controls flooding by using automatic gates that respond to the tides and how much it rains.

Did you know that smart cities use sustainable building materials to reduce their environmental impact?

Smart garbage trucks do selective waste collection, only emptying full bins.

Recycled materials are used to make new things.

A waste recycling center.

WASTE MANAGEMENT

In smart cities, waste is handled using innovative solutions. Special sensors in garbage bins tell collection trucks when they're full, so trucks only visit bins that need emptying. This saves fuel and time.

Some cities are developing underground vacuum systems that move trash through pipes to central waste collection centers or advanced recycling centers, where they use smart machines that automatically sort different recyclable materials.

Food scraps from homes and restaurants can be turned into compost for gardens. In some places, plastic bottles are repurposed into benches or playground equipment.

These systems help keep streets cleaner and reduce the total amount of waste that needs to be put into landfills.

In Seoul, they have these cool solar-powered trash cans that squash trash down and even tell the garbage collectors when they're full! They also have a "pay-as-you-throw" system where people pay for their trash based on how heavy it is, so everyone tries to recycle and compost more.

Smart displays on city infrastructure show residents how resources are used and encourage conservation.

Sensors using smart technology allow cities to show residents their utility usage in real time.

UTILITIES

Utility systems in smart cities work together to make sure everything runs well.

Smart water systems can find leaks right away, smart power systems are always changing to keep the lights on, and gas systems are constantly checking for safety issues.

Smart meters help people track their water and energy use, showing them ways to save resources and reduce bills. When problems occur, repair teams know exactly where to go to fix them quickly.

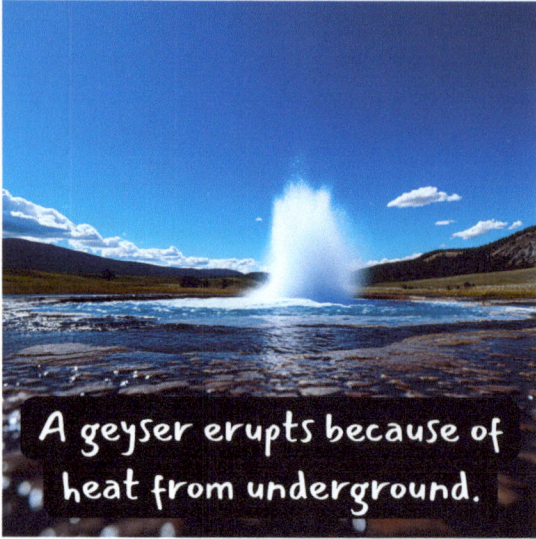
A geyser erupts because of heat from underground.

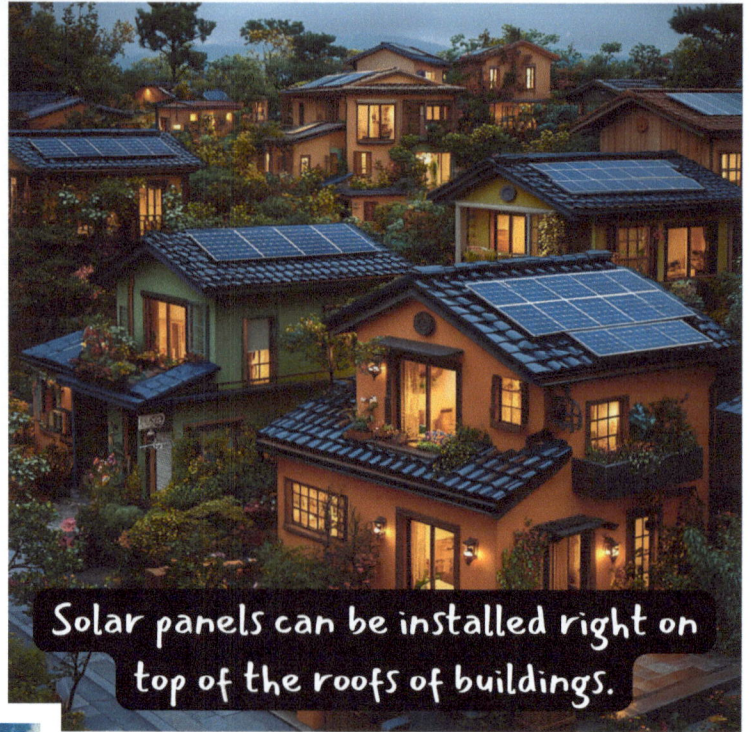
Solar panels can be installed right on top of the roofs of buildings.

Wind turbines don't look nice, but they can create a lot of energy.

Did you know that many smart cities offer mobile apps that let residents track their energy and water usage and receive personalized tips for saving resources?

SUSTAINABLE ENERGY

Sustainable energy is energy that comes from sources that won't run out. In smart cities, solar panels on rooftops catch sunlight and change it into electricity.

Wind turbines can also generate power from the wind, and in some cities, heat from the earth, also called geothermal heat, is used as an energy source.

In Amsterdam, the Johan Cruijff Arena is a sports stadium that uses 4,200 solar panels and has a huge energy storage system made from recycled electric car batteries. This powers the stadium when sporting events are happening, and when they have extra energy, they can share it with the surrounding neighborhoods.

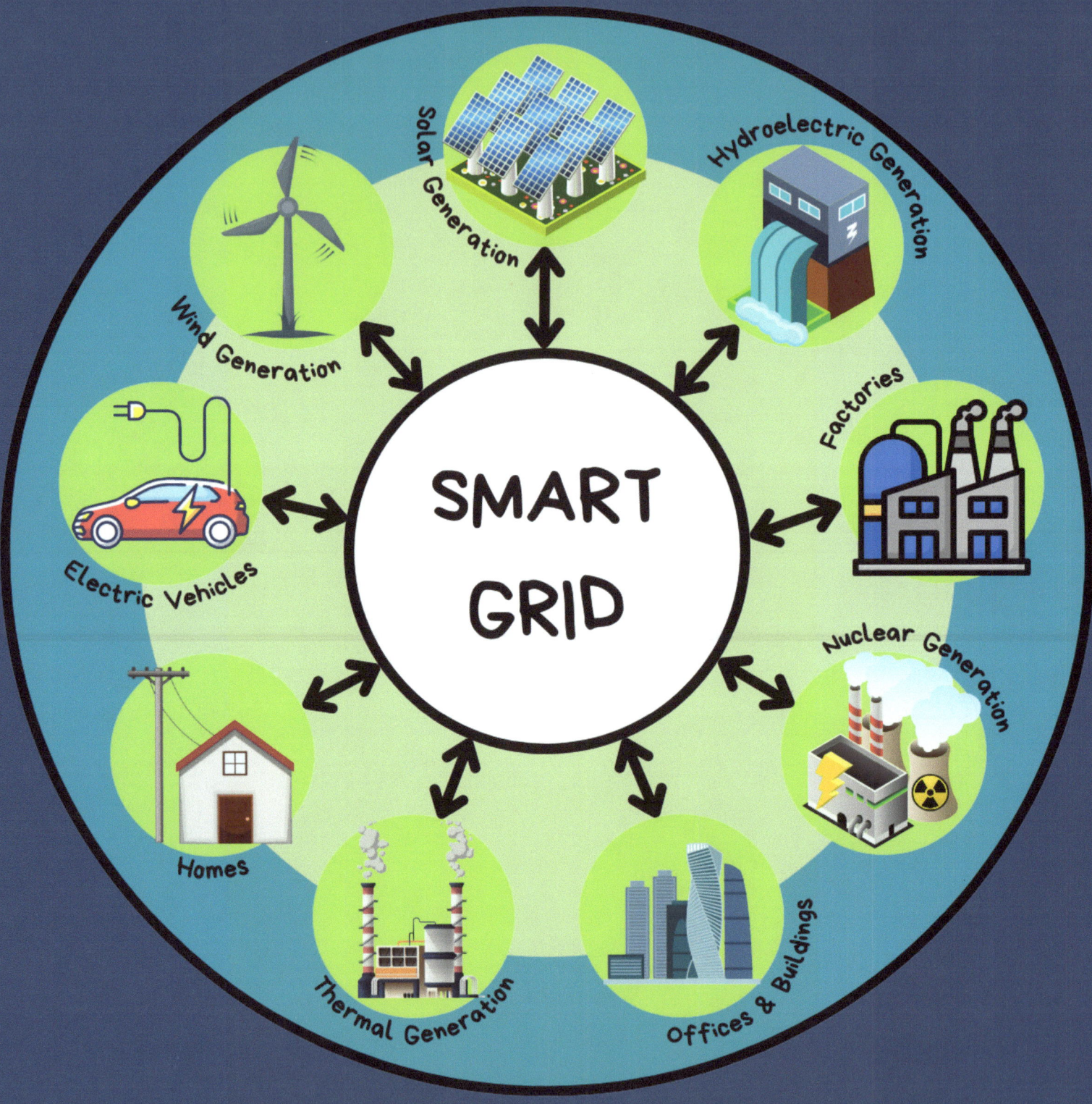

SMART GRID

Solar Generation

Hydroelectric Generation

Wind Generation

Factories

Electric Vehicles

Nuclear Generation

Homes

Offices & Buildings

Thermal Generation

THE POWER GRID

A smart electric grid is an advanced electricity network that makes everything about electricity, how it's made, how it's distributed, and how it's used, way better and more dependable.

The smart grid is like the city's power control center. It manages electricity use throughout the city, making sure power goes where it's needed most. When lots of people use electricity at once, the grid can adjust to prevent blackouts.

Solar panels and wind turbines connect to the smart grid, sharing clean energy across the city. Buildings with extra power can share it with other buildings, making the whole city more energy efficient.

A smart grid has sensors that can monitor energy use in real-time, so it can handle changes in demand, find problems, and even fix things on its own.

Keeping an eye on potential dangers can help stop disasters before they happen.

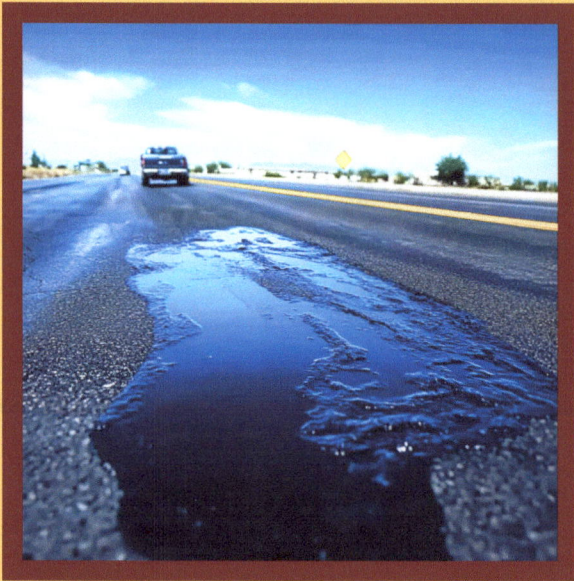

Oil spills should be cleaned up as soon as possible.

Smart fire detection systems help fire departments respond to fires before they spread through the community.

ENVIRONMENTAL MONITORING

Environmental sensors throughout the city keep track of air quality, noise levels, and weather conditions. This information helps city planners make decisions that protect people's health and the environment.

It can also spot when accidents cause damage, like oil spills or fires. It can direct emergency response services to these areas to reduce the risk of potential environmental disasters.

Smart systems can change traffic patterns to reduce air pollution levels. During storms, sensors monitor water levels to prevent flooding and keep people safe.

Virtual reality glasses.

A digital whiteboard in a school classroom.

An interactive exhibit in a museum.

A digital display in a library.

EDUCATION

Learning happens everywhere in smart cities, not just schools. Educational programs and internet access are available for free at digital learning hubs.

Smart classrooms use virtual reality systems to let students explore historical sites, conduct science experiments, and learn about different cultures without leaving their classrooms.

Interactive displays in museums and libraries respond to visitors' interests, making learning fun and personal.

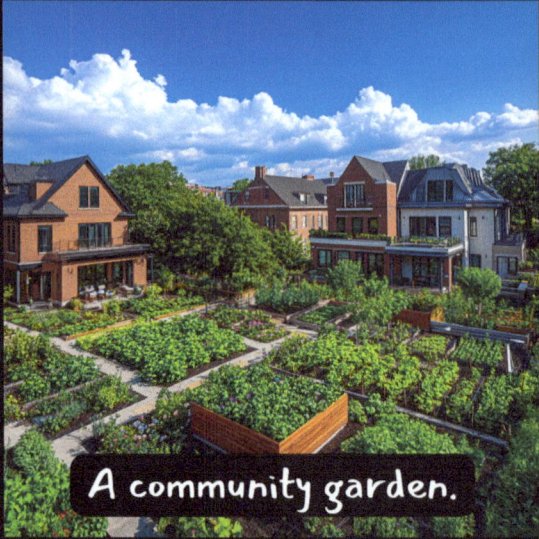

A community garden.

Rooftop gardens provide green spaces where people living in big cities enjoy the outdoors.

Indoor farms produce fresh produce right where they are needed.

Did you know that some smart cities use hydroponic systems where plants grow without soil, floating in nutrient-rich water instead?

URBAN AGRICULTURE

Smart cities grow food in creative ways, including vertical farms built indoors in tall buildings. They use special lights and automated watering systems, using less water than traditional farming. In these farm buildings, fresh food is produced close to where people live.

On residential buildings, rooftop gardens help feed communities while keeping buildings cool.

Community gardens use cool technology like sensors to keep an eye on soil health and how plants are growing. It's a great way to learn about growing food sustainably!

HEALTHCARE

Modern healthcare systems in smart cities use technology to keep people healthy.

Telemedicine systems let doctors help patients through video calls, especially those who live far away from hospitals or have trouble traveling.

Health monitoring systems track public health patterns and alert officials if many people in one area get sick. Smart ambulances use traffic data to reach people faster during emergencies.

Mobile apps allow
residents to access city
services remotely.

People can access city
information in real- time
using digital information
boards.

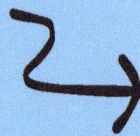

CITIZEN ENGAGEMENT

Smart cities make it easy for people to participate in making their community better. Mobile apps let residents report problems like broken streetlights or potholes directly to the City.

Digital voting systems help people share their opinions about new projects in their neighborhoods, while community information boards display real-time data about air quality, traffic conditions, and upcoming events.

This helps everyone stay informed and involved in making their city a better place to live.

Traffic lights adjust automatically to make traffic flow better.

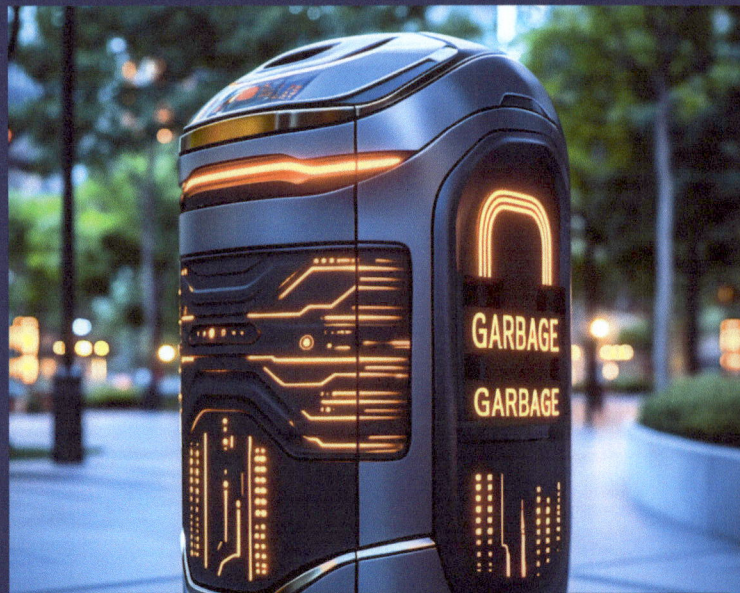

Garbage bins order their collection once they're full.

You can charge your laptop or access the internet from a smart park bench.

Street lights dim or switch off when no one is around.

THE INTERNET OF THINGS

Smart cities are filled with sensors. Sensors are like tiny computers that collect information throughout the city. They help monitor air quality, keep an eye on traffic patterns, and even determine when city parks need watering.

Street lights know when to turn on and off, trash bins signal when they need emptying, and water pipes can detect leaks before they become problems. Smart park benches can be provided with phone charging outlets and free internet access.

All these connected devices work together like a giant, helpful brain.

Cities protect their digital networks from people trying to access them illegally.

Cities need fancy computers to run all their services.

Cybersecurity protects networks from online attacks.

Hackers use their skills to access networks illegally to steal information.

CYBERSECURITY

In a smart city, it's very important to keep information safe. Special computer systems are used to protect the city's digital networks from bad people trying to access them without permission.

These security systems are always working to keep personal information private and make sure that city services run smoothly. Regular security updates and keeping an eye on things help stop problems before they start. This makes sure that smart city tech stays safe and works well for everyone.

Think of it this way. When you are playing online games with your friends, you don't want strangers to access your personal information since they may break into your game and delete all your progress. For the same reason, smart cities protect their information so hackers can't steal it.

Smart cities keep us connected to the internet wherever we go.

Digital information kiosks keep us informed of everything that happens in the city.

Libraries connect to the internet to bring us the most current information on any topic.

Did you know that community-based mobile apps allow residents to instantly report issues like potholes, broken streetlights, or graffiti?

DIGITAL CONNECTIVITY

Smart cities stay connected through networks of fiber-optic cables and wireless signals. Public Wi-Fi in parks, libraries, and buses helps people stay connected wherever they go.

Information kiosks in public spaces help people learn about city services, find directions, or call for help in emergencies.

Libraries and community centers offer online or digital learning programs to help everyone understand and use new technology.

A digital access card

Did you know, that in smart cities, your digital identity can help doctors and hospitals take better care of you during emergencies?

Did you know, that digital identity in smart cities can be used to create personalized services for kids, like automatically adjusting library recommendations based on your interests, or suggesting after-school activities nearby that match your hobbies?

Paying for public services with a mobile app is faster and more convenient.

DIGITAL IDENTITY

Secure digital systems allow citizens to access city services in smart cities easily. Special cards or mobile apps let people ride buses, enter libraries, and use community centers.

These digital IDs keep personal information safe while making it convenient to use city services.

The same system helps people pay for parking, check out library books, and register for community programs. Everything is connected, making city life easier and organized.

Again, it's very important to protect your digital identity. Never share your personal information, like usernames and passwords, with anyone except Mom and Dad.

Smart sensors are placed throughout the city.

Cameras make sure traffic flows efficiently and safely.

Robots are being developed to do the jobs people don't want.

Special robots are used to do bridge inspections.

ARTIFICIAL INTELLIGENCE AND ROBOTICS

By using artificial intelligence (AI), cities make different systems run by themselves without people controlling them.

Cities use AI to study the information collected from special sensors placed all throughout the city. They then use this information to decide where to build new roads or bike lanes, find the best locations for open spaces or parks, or predict where new schools might be needed.

Smart traffic lights use AI to adjust their timing based on traffic patterns at different times of the day.

Robots help maintain city infrastructure by inspecting bridges, cleaning solar panels, and fixing problems in underground pipes.

When these technologies are used to perform some of the more repetitive tasks, city workers can concentrate on more important city improvements.

DISASTER PREVENTION

Smart cities have really cool tech that can predict natural disasters like storms and floods. They use things like weather stations and water sensors to spot the early signs of trouble. This gives people a heads-up so they can stay safe in emergencies.

Resilience centers are special buildings that have backup power and communications systems. These centers can be used to help coordinate response teams and provide safe spaces for people to gather during emergencies.

Did you know that some smart cities use robots and drones to help with emergency response? Robots can enter dangerous buildings to provide aid, deliver supplies, and locate people using thermal cameras, and drones can fly over emergencies to help first responders better assess the dangers.

Monitoring systems can warn us when severe weather comes our way.

Network servers with backup power keep working when there's a power outage.

A smart fire detector.

EMERGENCY RESPONSE

Emergency response systems in smart cities use cool tech like smart sensors and cameras to find the fastest routes for ambulances and fire trucks. They can change traffic lights automatically to get them there faster and save lives.

Weather monitoring systems can predict storms and flooding, giving people early warnings and more time to respond to natural disasters.

Fire sensors in buildings can detect smoke and heat before flames appear.

Resilience centers have backup power and communication systems to make sure everything keeps working in the case of an emergency. Some cities even use drones to check out dangerous situations before sending in first responders.

Mobile apps provide real-time traffic conditions, alert residents about emergencies and inform residents of air quality concerns.

Cities provide digital service centers for residents who don't have access to technology.

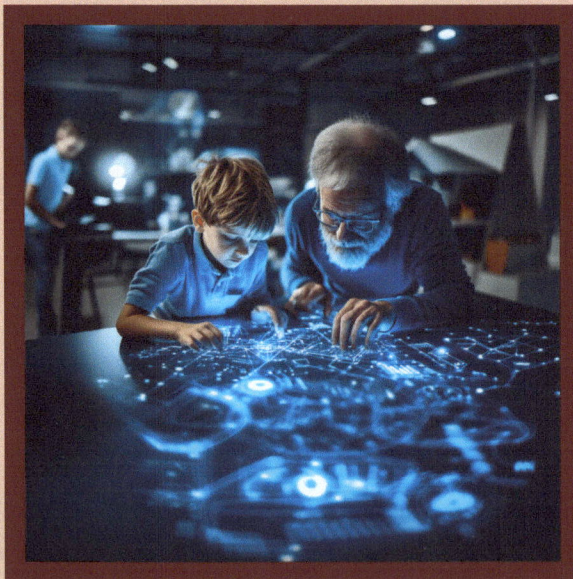

Cities provide training opportunities, where young and old can learn together about the benefits of smart technologies.

COMMUNITY SUPPORT

Smart cities have digital service centers that help people find jobs, places to live, and other things they need. They even have apps that connect volunteers with community projects and help neighbors share tools and supplies.

Special programs teach everyone, even older folks and people with disabilities, how to use smart technology. Cities want to ensure everyone can keep up in this digital world!

Smart cities show us how technology can make urban life better for everyone. From cleaner air to safer streets, smarter buildings to better transportation, these innovations help create communities where people and nature can thrive together.

By working together and using tech responsibly, we can tackle problems and create opportunities that benefit everyone. The future of our cities depends on finding innovative ways to use technology while protecting our environment at the same time.

Today, we showed you only a few examples of how technology helps cities run efficiently. There are many more examples of smart technologies. Take a look around your city and discover how technology is improving your lives.

Smart cities of the future will need imaginative thinkers like you to dream up innovative solutions and create an even better tomorrow.

So long, friends! We hope to see you all again soon!

Smart Cities Glossary

A <u>glossary</u> is like a mini-dictionary of terms with definitions.

Here's a glossary of terms used for <u>Smart Cities</u>.

<u>5G</u> - The newest generation of wireless internet that makes devices and systems in a smart city work faster and more reliably.

<u>Artificial Intelligence (AI)</u> - Computer programs that learn and make decisions on their own. In smart cities, AI helps manage things like traffic signals and city planning by analyzing data from sensors.

<u>Augmented Reality (AR)</u> - Technology that overlays digital information onto the real world, often used for interactive learning experiences or city planning.

<u>Autonomous Vehicles</u> - Self-driving vehicles that use cameras, sensors, and AI to navigate roads safely without a human driver.

<u>Big Data</u> - Large amounts of information collected from various sources (like sensors and cameras) that cities analyze to understand trends and improve services.

<u>Cloud Computing</u> - Using powerful computers and storage over the internet to process and store the vast amounts of data that a smart city generates.

<u>Citizen Engagement</u> - Ways for citizens to share ideas, report issues, and work with city leaders, often through apps, to help improve their community.

Cybersecurity - Practices and tools used to protect digital systems from hackers and other threats, ensuring personal data and city services remain safe.

Data Analytics - The process of examining large amounts of information to find patterns and insights that can help improve city services and planning.

Digital Connectivity - Networks, like Wi-Fi and fiber-optic cables, that keep devices and people connected so city services can work smoothly.

Digital Identity - A secure way for people to prove who they are online, often through special cards or apps, so they can safely access city services.

Digital Twin - A digital copy of a physical object or even an entire city used to run simulations and test improvements before making real-world changes.

Edge Computing - Processing data close to where it's collected (on sensors or local devices), allowing smart systems to respond more quickly without sending all the data to a central server.

E-Governance - The use of digital tools by governments to provide services, share information, and engage with citizens more efficiently.

Emergency Response - Systems that use technology, such as smart sensors and real-time data, to help emergency services quickly reach people in need during crises.

Green Buildings - Eco-friendly buildings with features like smart windows and automated systems that help control indoor temperatures and reduce energy waste.

Intelligent Transportation Systems (ITS) - High-tech systems that make transportation safer and more efficient by using data and communication between vehicles and infrastructure.

Internet of Things (IoT) - A network of everyday devices, like sensors, smart lights, and appliances, that connect to the internet and share information to work together smarter.

Machine Learning - A branch of AI where computers learn from data, improving tasks like predicting traffic or managing energy use over time.

Mobility as a Service (MaaS) - An approach that combines various transportation services (buses, trains, bikes, rideshares) into one accessible service via a single app.

Renewable Energy - Energy produced from natural sources like sunlight or wind, which are naturally replenished and help reduce reliance on fossil fuels.

Resilience Centers - Special buildings equipped with backup power and communication systems to keep essential services running during emergencies like storms or floods.

<u>Sensors</u> - Small devices that collect information (such as temperature, air quality, or traffic levels) to help the city monitor conditions and react quickly.

<u>Smart City</u> - A city that uses technology and connected systems to improve everyday life by making services like transportation and energy more efficient.

<u>Smart City Platform</u> - A digital system that gathers data from various parts of the city, helping to manage services and make decisions that improve quality of life.

<u>Smart Grid</u> - An advanced electricity network that uses sensors and computers to balance energy use, prevent blackouts, and deliver power where it's needed most.

<u>Smart Infrastructure</u> - Technology-enhanced structures like buildings, roads, and bridges that are monitored and maintained using digital tools to keep them safe and efficient.

<u>Smart Lighting</u> - Lighting systems that automatically adjust brightness based on movement or time of day to save energy and enhance safety.

<u>Smart Transportation</u> - Modern systems that use technology to optimize buses, trains, self-driving vehicles, and bikes by finding the best routes and adjusting schedules.

<u>Sustainable Development</u> - Designing and building cities in ways that meet current needs without compromising the ability of future generations to meet theirs.

Sustainable Energy - Energy derived from natural sources that won't run out, like sunlight, wind, or geothermal heat, helping reduce pollution and protect the environment.

Telemedicine - The use of video calls and digital tools to connect doctors and patients, making healthcare more accessible, especially for those far from hospitals.

Urban Agriculture - Innovative ways to grow food in cities, such as rooftop gardens or vertical farms, which provide fresh, local produce and promote sustainability.

Urban Informatics - The study of how technology, data, and design can improve the planning and operation of cities.

Waste Management - Efficient and environmentally friendly handling of trash using sensors and automated systems to collect, sort, recycle, or dispose of waste.

Water Management - Using technology to monitor water quality, detect leaks early, and manage water usage to conserve this precious resource.

Smart Cities Quiz

1. What best describes a smart city?
    a) A city with lots of parks.
    b) A city that uses technology to improve everyday life.
    c) A city with only old buildings.
    d) A city that only uses manual systems.

2. Which system in a smart city helps reduce traffic jams?
    a) Smart lighting.
    b) Smart transportation.
    c) Digital identity.
    d) Urban agriculture.

3. What is one function of smart windows in green buildings?
    a) Letting people see inside.
    b) Regulating indoor temperatures by reducing heat loss.
    c) Changing colors for decoration.
    d) Generating electricity.

4. Self-driving vehicles navigate safely using which of the following?
    a) Magnetic sensors.
    b) Cameras and sensors.
    c) Solar panels.
    d) Manual steering.

5. How do smart parking systems assist drivers?
    a) They guide drivers to available parking spots.
    b) They repair vehicles.
    c) They provide entertainment.
    d) They alert drivers about weather changes.

6. What is the main benefit of smart lighting?
    a) It uses more energy
    b) It changes colors randomly
    c) It saves energy and increases safety
    d) It only operates during the day

7. How do smart water meters help residents?
    a) By cleaning the water automatically
    b) By measuring water temperature
    c) By helping people understand and manage their water usage
    d) By increasing water pressure

8. What role do sensors play in a smart city?
    a) They light up streets
    b) They collect environmental data like air quality and traffic levels
    c) They build roads
    d) They replace digital identity systems

9. Which system uses digital tools to help emergency services reach people faster?
    a) Smart grid
    b) Emergency response systems
    c) Urban agriculture
    d) Digital connectivity

10. What is one purpose of a smart electric grid?
    a) To provide public Wi-Fi
    b) To manage electricity use and prevent blackouts
    c) To monitor water quality
    d) To control self-driving vehicles

11. A _____ city is one that uses technology and connected systems to improve everyday life.

12. In a smart city, _____ systems adjust traffic signals based on how many cars are waiting.

13. Green buildings often have _____ windows that help regulate indoor temperatures.

14. Sensors in a smart city collect data about the environment, such as air quality, _____ levels, and water leaks.

15. Special sensors in garbage bins let collection trucks know when they are _____.

16. Self-driving vehicles use _____ and sensors to navigate safely.

17. The advanced electricity network in a smart city is called a _____ grid.

18. _____ identity allows citizens to access city services securely using digital tools.

19. Telemedicine uses video calls to connect _____ and patients.

20. Vertical farms and rooftop gardens are examples of urban _____.

21. Smart cities only use technology for entertainment purposes.

22. Sensors are used in smart cities to collect environmental data such as air quality and water leaks.

23. Self-driving vehicles rely solely on human drivers to navigate safely.

24. Smart lighting systems adjust brightness based on movement to save energy.

25. Waste management in smart cities uses automated systems to improve efficiency.

26. Digital connectivity in a smart city relies on networks like Wi-Fi and fiber-optic cables.

27. A smart grid helps prevent blackouts by managing electricity usage in real-time.

28. Urban agriculture in smart cities is limited to traditional farming methods.

29. Telemedicine makes healthcare more accessible by connecting doctors and patients through digital tools.

30. Citizen engagement in smart cities involves only voting in elections.

Smart Cities Quiz - Answer Key

Multiple Choice	Fill in the Blank	True/False
1. b	11. smart	21. False
2. b	12. transportation	22. True
3. b	13. smart	23. False
4. b	14. traffic	24. True
5. a	15. full	25. True
6. c	16. cameras	26. True
7. c	17. smart	27. True
8. b	18. Digital	28. False
9. b	19. doctors	29. True
10. b	20. agriculture	30. False

Take a look at other subjects Lila and Andy are learning about...

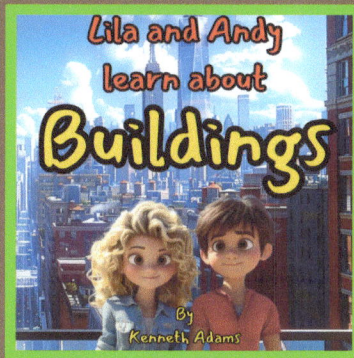

Lila and Andy learn about **Buildings**
By Kenneth Adams

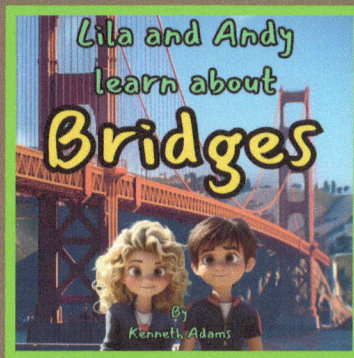

Lila and Andy learn about **Bridges**
By Kenneth Adams

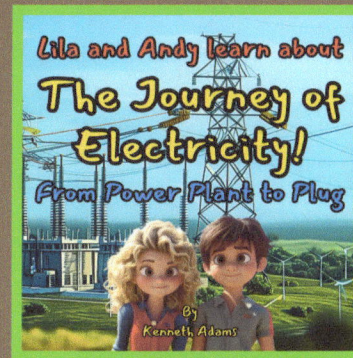

Lila and Andy learn about **The Journey of Electricity!**
From Power Plant to Plug
By Kenneth Adams

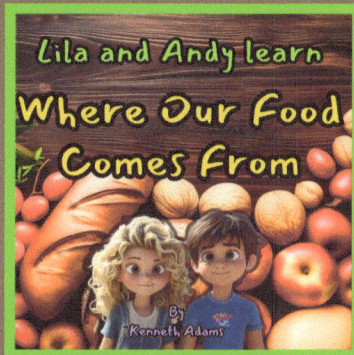

Lila and Andy learn **Where Our Food Comes From**
By Kenneth Adams

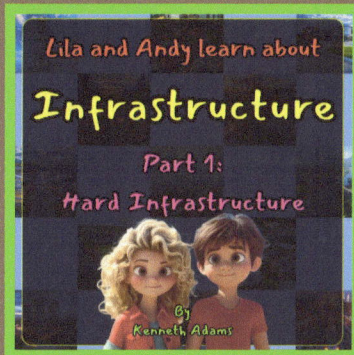

Lila and Andy learn about **Infrastructure**
Part 1: Hard Infrastructure
By Kenneth Adams

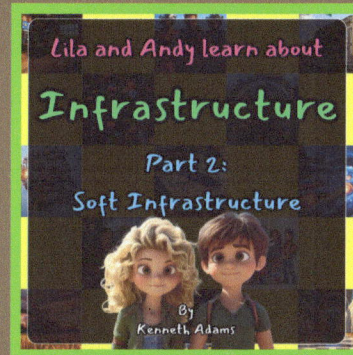

Lila and Andy learn about **Infrastructure**
Part 2: Soft Infrastructure
By Kenneth Adams

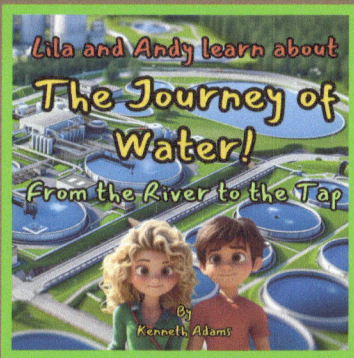

Lila and Andy learn about **The Journey of Water!**
From the River to the Tap
By Kenneth Adams

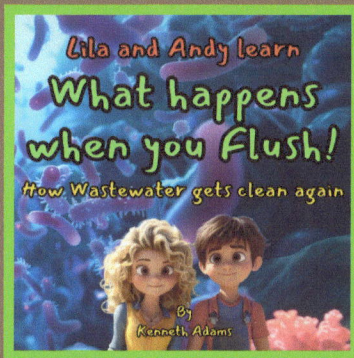

Lila and Andy learn **What happens when you Flush!**
How Wastewater gets clean again
By Kenneth Adams

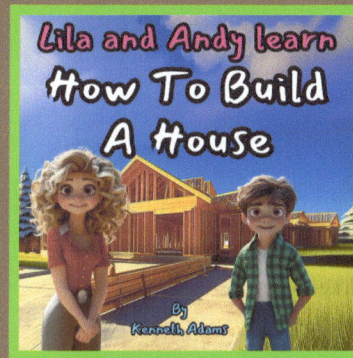

Lila and Andy learn **How To Build A House**
By Kenneth Adams

Lila and Andy learn about **Recycling**

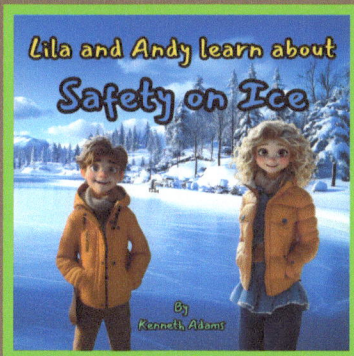

Lila and Andy learn about **Safety on Ice**
By Kenneth Adams

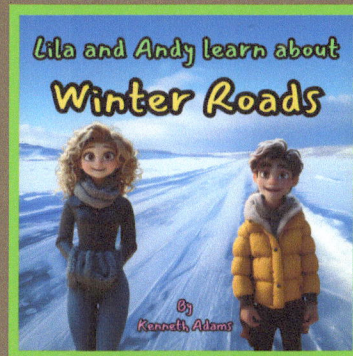

Lila and Andy learn about **Winter Roads**
By Kenneth Adams

www.ingramcontent.com/pod-product-compliance
Lightning Source LLC
Chambersburg PA
CBHW040915100426

42737CB00042B/90